MARS

PLANETS IN OUR SOLAR SYSTEM

CHILDREN'S ASTRONOMY EDITION

SPEEDY
PUBLISHING

Speedy Publishing LLC
40 E. Main St. #1156
Newark, DE 19711
www.speedypublishing.com

The planet is named after Mars, the Roman god of war.

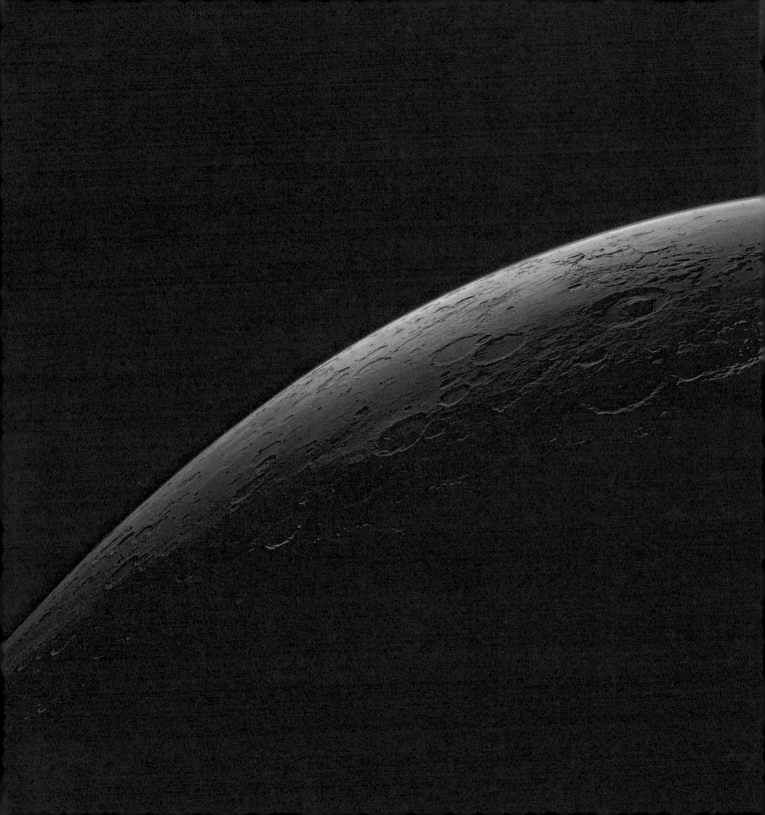

Mars is
the fourth
planet from
the Sun and
the second
smallest
planet in the
Solar System.

Mars experiences violent dust storms which continually change its surface.

Mars is sometimes called the Red Planet because it is covered with rust-like dust.

Mars is host to seven functioning spacecrafts, five in orbit and two on the surface.

Mars is a terrestrial planet and has a very thin atmosphere made mostly of carbon dioxide.

Mars has many channels, plains and canyons on the surface which could have been caused by water erosion in the past.

Mars has both North and South polar ice caps, both ice caps are made mostly of frozen water.

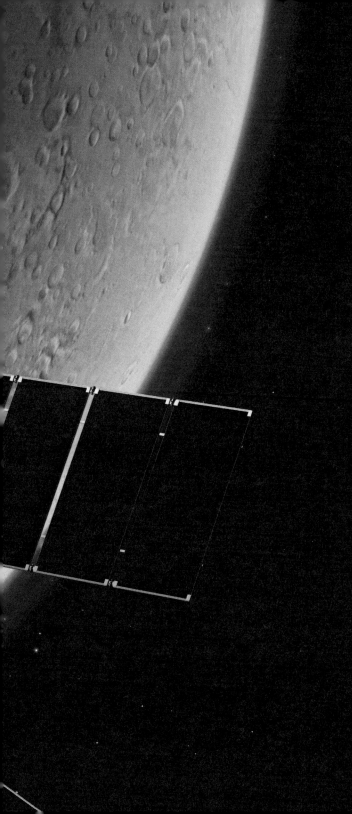

Temperature in Venus ranges from -120 Degrees Celsius on winter to 25 Degrees Celsius in the summer.

Mars has many channels, plains and canyons on the surface which could have been caused by water erosion in the past.

Mars has seasons like Earth too, due to the similar tilts of the two planets' rotational axes.

Mars is home to the tallest mountain in the solar system. The Olympus Mons, a shield volcano, is 21km high and 600km in diameter.

A Martian
year is equal
to I year, 320
days, and
18.2 hours
on Earth.

Mars is also home to the largest known canyon, Valles Marineris, in the Solar System.

Mars has two moons, Phobos and Deimos. Both moons are made of carbon-rich rock mixed with ice.

Mars does not have a magnetic field.

Mars is located closer to the asteroid belt, so it has an increased chance of being struck by materials from that source.

Pieces of Mars
have been
found on Earth.

Made in United States
North Haven, CT
14 March 2023